Table of Contents

Introduction		3
Chapter 1:	Tapping into Personal Vision and Purpose	5
Chapter 2:	Reflecting on Personal Values and Principles	23
Chapter 3:	Crafting a Personal Mission Statement	36
Chapter 4:	Setting SMART Goals	43
Chapter 5:	Prioritizing Based on Impact	52
Chapter 6	Creating a Weekly Schedule	60
Chapter 7:	Creating a Weekly Schedule	66
Chapter 8:	Continuous Learning and Personal Development	78

Chapter 9:	The Benefits of Regular Self-Assessment and Reflection	88
Chapter 10:	Emotional Intelligence and Self-Awareness	96
Chapter 11	Book Conclusion	104

Appendices

Appendix A:	Developing Your Personal Vision	108
Appendix B:	Setting Effective Goals	111
Appendix C:	Optimizing Personal Effectiveness	57
Appendix D:	Growth and Development	116
Recommended Resources:		118
Further media Resources:		119

Mastering Personal Effectiveness:
A Comprehensive Guide to Personal Growth and Success

Introduction:

What does it mean to be truly effective in life? How can we maximize our potential and live up to our capabilities each day? This book dives deeply into the world of personal effectiveness to help you do just that.
Within these pages, we'll explore what it takes to perform at your peak—professionally, socially, physically, mentally, and emotionally. You'll learn research-backed strategies to become more productive, motivated, organized, and focused. We'll cover how to set meaningful goals, manage time wisely, overcome procrastination, and boost productivity so you can accomplish more of what matters most.

Beyond work, we'll discuss how to apply personal effectiveness principles to enhance your

relationships, improve your well-being, pursue fulfilling hobbies, and generally get the most out of each moment. When you operate at your highest levels of energy, clarity, and drive on a consistent basis, extraordinary things become possible.
The benefits of developing strong personal effectiveness extend to all aspects of life. With the insights you'll gain here, you can step up as a leader at work, be fully present with loved ones, establish healthy habits, tackle new challenges, and bring passion and purpose to each day. Investing in yourself pays dividends that will compound exponentially over your lifetime.

The journey begins here. Let's explore what it means to fully activate your potential! By committing to continual self-improvement, you can achieve the happiness, success, and fulfilment you desire.

Chapter 1.

Tapping into Personal Vision and Purpose.

Having a clear sense of vision and purpose in life is foundational to personal effectiveness. When you know what matters most to you and what you want to accomplish, you can make intentional choices that align with those priorities each day. In this chapter, we'll explore ways to get in touch with your core values, define an inspiring vision for your future, and understand your life's purpose. With this clarity, you'll be equipped to set goals and make decisions that help you maximize your potential.

Defining Your Values

Your values are the core principles and beliefs that drive your choices and behaviours. They reflect what you care about most and provide an inner compass to guide you. When life gets busy, it's easy to lose connection with these essential values. That's why consciously defining them is so important. Here are some exercises to get clear on your values:

- Make a list of times when you felt truly fulfilled, motivated, and like you were making a difference. What values do these peak experiences reflect? Common values include integrity, growth, compassion, justice, creativity, community, family, spirituality, and health.
- Imagine you only have one week left to live. How would you spend your time? What relationships, activities, and goals would become most important? What this reveals about your values.
- Reflect on people you admire. What values do they embody that you resonate with?
- Consider what you'd like people to say about you at your funeral. What qualities would you want them to highlight?

Once you've brainstormed, narrow your list down to your top 5-10 core values. Post them somewhere visible as a daily reminder to align your actions with what matters most. Revisiting this list annually allows you to evaluate if your priorities have shifted. When you make values-based choices, you'll feel more purposeful and fulfilled.

Crafting Your Vision

With your values clarified, the next step is defining your vision - an inspiring mental image of your desired future. This could relate to your career, relationships, self-development, lifestyle, or any aspect of life that energizes you. A compelling vision serves as a North Star guiding your goals and daily choices. It expands your sense of possibility and fuels motivation.

To craft your vision:

- Imagine yourself 5-10 years from now. What does your ideal life look like? Picture it in vivid detail - where you live, what you do, who you spend time with, daily habits and routines, etc.
- What experiences and accomplishments would bring you deep satisfaction? See yourself achieving them.
- What impact do you want to make in the world or people's lives? How can you live your values?

- What skills, qualities, or mind-sets does your future self have? Incorporate developing those into your vision.

Write your vision down in an inspirational paragraph or letter to your future self. Revisit it often and continue to refine it as your dreams evolve. Share it with supportive loved ones to make it feel more real. With consistent effort over time, you can progress toward making this vision a reality.

Understanding Your Purpose

Your life purpose encompasses the unique gifts and talents you're meant to offer the world. It extends beyond personal wants to consider how to be of service to others. Discovering your purpose involves looking both within and beyond yourself. Here are some key elements that give clues to your purpose:

- Passions - What energizes and excites you? When do you lose track of time? What interests have stayed with you since childhood?

- Talents - What natural strengths and abilities do you have? What skills come easily? What do people often compliment you on?
- Values - How do you most want to express your core values? What issues do you care about?
- Personality - What personality traits best equip you to serve and add value? Are you inspiring, supportive, driven, creative?
- Experiences - What life experiences have shaped you? How could you use your knowledge to help others with similar struggles?
- Needs - What unmet needs in the world align with your abilities? What problems or gaps could you reasonably help fill?
- Impact - What legacy do you want to leave behind? How can you positively influence your family, community, or the world?

Finding the connective thread between these elements will reveal the essence of your purpose. This may take deep self-reflection. Be patient and listen to your intuition. When your work aligns with your purpose, you'll feel imbued with greater meaning.

Defining Goals and Making Plans

With your vision and purpose clarified, you can set focused goals and make detailed plans to reach them. Approach goal-setting as a process rather than a one-time event. Here are steps for effective goal planning:

- Break your vision into actionable goals for the next 1, 3, and 5 years. Make goals specific, measurable, achievable, relevant, and time-bound.
- Break annual goals into quarterly, monthly, and weekly objectives. Define concrete steps to achieve each.
- Make plans flexible, not rigid. Update and adjust goals as needed based on changing circumstances.
- Align goals with your core values and purpose to stay motivated. Know why each matters.
- Account for relationships, self-care, recreation, and self-development. Don't sacrifice them for work goals alone.

- Tell supportive friends and family about your goals to build accountability.
- Anticipate obstacles, distractions, and competing aims that may arise. Strategize ways to overcome them.
- Use goal tracking apps, journals, or calendars to monitor progress and stay on track.

With strategic goal planning, you can build momentum each day that takes you where you truly want to go in life. Review and revise goals regularly to sustain focus as you evolve.

Cultivating Metacognition

Metacognition simply means thinking about your thinking. It's the ability to step back and look at your thought processes from a higher perspective. When you can examine your own mind, you gain power over it. You can consciously direct your thoughts rather than letting them control you. Metacognition allows you to monitor unhelpful thinking patterns and intentionally shift to more empowering ones. Here's how to cultivate it:

- Pause throughout the day to observe your thoughts non-judgmentally. What emotions are present? How rational are your thought processes?
- Question limiting beliefs and self-talk. Ask yourself if they're grounded in reality or past conditioning. Seek alternative perspectives.
- Identify distortions like all-or-nothing thinking, catastrophic predictions, or exaggerating negatives. Counter them with more balanced thoughts.

- Notice when strong emotions influence your thinking. Name the emotion and consider if it's disproportionate to the situation.
- Before reacting to stressors, take a few deep breaths. Create space between the trigger and your response.
- Reflect on why you make certain decisions. Are you overly influenced by the past, other's expectations, or trying to avoid discomfort?
- Consider your core values and bigger picture priorities. How do your current thoughts align or misalign?

With regular metacognitive check-ins, you gain freedom from limiting thought patterns. This clarity of thinking allows you to consciously create your life rather than reactively drift through it.

Evaluating Your Locus of Control

Your locus of control refers to how much power you believe you have over your life circumstances. Those with an internal locus of control generally believe their actions shape outcomes. Those with an external locus attribute events to external factors like luck or destiny.

An internal locus fosters self-efficacy and motivation. When you take personal responsibility, you directly impact results rather than feeling like a helpless victim. Realistically assessing your locus of control in different situations allows you to spot where to take more initiative.

Ask yourself:

- In what areas of life do I feel empowered versus powerless? Why?
- Do I acknowledge my strong and weak points or blame only external factors for setbacks?
- Am I proactive or passive when faced with problems? Do I get creative or give up easily?
- How decisive or indecisive am I when making choices? Do I delay due to fear of failure?
- When plans get derailed, do I problem solve solutions or disengage?
- Am I resilient in the face of hardship? Do I dwell on misfortunes or bounce back?
- Do I network, ask for help, and build key relationships or remain isolated?

- Do I take care of my physical and mental health or neglect self-care?

With radical self-honesty, you can determine where to take more ownership in your life. Small acts of agency compound to make you feel able to accomplish great things.

Defeating Perfectionism

For many, perfectionism derails progress rather than fuels it. Trying to do everything flawlessly becomes paralyzing. You may put off tasks forever because you can't meet unrealistic standards. Or you might redo work repeatedly, never feeling it's good enough. Perfectionism often stems from underlying insecurity or fear of failure. The desire to control how everything turns out backfires.
Combat perfectionism with these strategies:

- Identify core fears driving it, like disappointing others or not feeling competent. Address them directly.
- Focus on learning and growth rather than perfect outcomes. Progress requires mistakes.

- Break large goals into smaller steps. Complete them one mini-milestone at a time.
- Prioritize what really needs perfection versus what just needs completion. Don't over-invest energy.
- Set deadlines to finish work rather than agonizing indefinitely until it feels right.
- Celebrate effort and consistency. Don't just reward yourself for flawlessness.
- Remember tasks don't define your worth. Doing something imperfectly isn't failing as a person.

By letting go of rigid ideals, you can take action aligned with your capabilities each day. Excellence comes from regularly showing up and doing your best.

Conquering Procrastination.

Procrastination involves voluntarily delaying important tasks despite knowing there will be negative consequences. It often stems from feeling overwhelmed by a big project and not knowing where to begin. Or you may use procrastination to avoid discomfort like boredom, uncertainty, or hard work. This gives temporary relief but increases stress long-term when deadlines loom.

Try these methods to overcome procrastination:

- Break large projects into bite-sized daily tasks so momentum builds.
- Batch similar tasks like phone calls together to be efficient.
- Schedule tasks during your peak energy times when focus comes easier.
- Eliminate distractions like email or social media during work time.
- Join an accountability buddy or mastermind group to report your progress.
- Notice when you procrastinate and why. Address the root causes.
- Reward yourself for timely completion rather than starting tasks.
- Don't wait for motivation. Discipline leads to motivation.
- Be gentle with yourself if you get off track. Just restart as soon as possible.

With consistent effort to show up each day, substantial progress gets made. Procrastination loses its grip as you build work momentum.
Organizing Your Environment

Your physical environment impacts your mental clarity and productivity immensely. When your space is chaotic, your mind absorbs that energy. An organized, optimized workspace helps you conserve mental bandwidth for deep focus and creative thinking.

To organize your environment:

- Declutter frequently. Get rid of what you don't use or need. Have a place for everything.
- Let go of papers and items you can digitize. Back up files online for easy access.
- Use tools like planners, whiteboards, or project management software to stay on top of tasks.
- Minimize visual distractions and clutter. Consider a soothing, minimalist look.

- Ensure your desk and chair enable proper ergonomics. Reduce pain that distracts.
- Incorporate plants, art, music, or elements that spark joy and reduce stress.
- Designate different work zones for tasks requiring quiet focus versus collaboration.
- Adjust lighting to be bright enough for detailed work but not cause eye strain.
- Experiment to find your ideal noise level. Some need silence while others prefer ambient sounds.

With thoughtful tweaks to your physical workspace, you'll be amazed at how much more efficiently you can work and think.

Boosting Daily Motivation

It's easy to start the day motivated but lose steam by the afternoon. When you notice energy lagging, it's time to inject a motivational booster shot. Here are quick ways to reignite your drive:

- Take a short walk or do jumping jacks to increase blood flow and oxygen to the brain.

- Drink water to prevent dehydration from sabotaging focus.
- Eat a healthy snack like nuts or fruit to balance blood sugar.
- Listen to uplifting music or a podcast to stimulate your mind.
- Look at vision boards with inspiring images and quotes.
- Review your long-term goals and why they matter.
- Scan your calendar to celebrate accomplished tasks.
- Text an accountability partner about what you'll achieve next.
- Recall past wins when you persevered through difficulty.
- Write down current thoughts cluttering your mind.

Purposeful breaks to recharge your battery keep your motivation muscles flexed. With renewed energy, tackle work with gusto.

Balancing Work and Rest

Hustle culture promotes the idea that highly productive people work nonstop. But in reality, quality rest is essential to performing at your best. Proper work-life balance reduces stress while enhancing focus, creativity, and stamina. Strive to integrate the following rest practices:

- Take a true lunch break each day to eat mindfully away from your desk.
- Establish workday stopping points. Power down at least an hour before bedtime.
- Set healthy boundaries and learn to say no if people ask for too much.
- Unplug with a "digital sundown" by limiting technology in the evenings.
- Observe how different types of recreation and socializing energize you. Do more of those.
- If you wake early, savor a slow morning routine before work.
- Schedule micro-breaks between intense work periods to recharge.
- Take all your vacation days. Disconnect completely at least once a year.

- Get adequate sleep based on your needs. Quality trumps quantity.

With strategic intervals of renewal, you'll tap into deeper energy reserves. You'll be amazed at how much more relaxed and productive you feel.

Chapter 2:
Reflecting on Personal Values and Principles

Our values and principles serve as an inner compass, guiding our choices and shaping our actions. When aligned with core values, life takes on greater meaning, purpose and direction. This chapter provides practical exercises to gain clarity on your values along with techniques to integrate them into daily life. By consciously defining and living your values, you can steer your life toward fulfilment.

Understanding Personal Values

Values represent our highest priorities and deeply held beliefs about what is right, important and meaningful. They reflect the essence of who we are at our core and point to our unique purpose in the world. Values encompass various life domains:

- Relationships - How we connect with others

- Growth & Contribution - How we challenge ourselves and uplift others

- Health & Wellbeing - How we care for our body, mind and spirit

- Integrity & Ethics - How we operate with honesty, authenticity and morality

- Community & Environment - How we positively engage with the world around us

- Achievement & Success - How we apply our talents to reach goals and serve society

- Spirituality & Meaning - How we find inner peace, wisdom and connection to the divine

Our values motivate us, bring joy and imbue life with meaning. They guide how we invest our limited time, energy and resources. When facing difficult dilemmas, our values point the way forward. They anchor us through hardships and humbly guide us through triumphs. Our values keep us aligned with life's essence.

Discovering Your Core Personal Values

With so many values to potentially integrate, how can you determine which resonate most deeply? The following reflective exercises can help identify your true north principles:

- Recall peak experiences when you felt aligned, joyful and fully yourself. What values do those moments reflect? What activities bring out your best self? If you felt that way more often, what would you do differently?

- Consider who and what you appreciate most in life. What do your loved ones, passions, possessions and sanctuaries represent? What makes you feel grounded?

- Remember difficult times when you demonstrated resilience. What values empowered you through challenges? What gave you strength and meaning?

- Envision your best possible self in 5-10 years. What principles guide your future growth? How do you positively contribute?

- Imagine you had one year left to live. How would you spend it? Who and what would matter most? What would give you comfort?

- What world issues inspire passion in you? What change would you like to see? How can you be part of the solution?

Once you review these reflections, narrow down 5-10 that form your core essence and align with your life vision. These values become your decision-making filter moving forward.

Assessing Alignment of Values and Actions

With core values defined, assess how consistently your current actions align. Observe your daily routines, habits, conversations and spending:

- Do you devote time and energy to activities linked to your values or less important matters?

- Do you prioritize self-care in line with your health values or neglect needs?

- Does your work fulfil your growth values or drain you?

- Do you model integrity through honesty and accountability or bend rules for convenience?

- Does your social circle share your values and bring out your best self?

- Do you spend money wisely on what matters or mindlessly consume?

- Do you uphold spiritual values like mindfulness and gratitude daily or just when remembered?

Misalignment between values and actions signals necessary change. If life feels adrift, you have drifted from your core. Reconnecting to your principles will reignite peace and purpose.

Setting Goals Aligned with Values

With clarified values, set goals exemplifying them so daily efforts build toward your vision. Ensure each goal aligns with core priorities by asking:

- How will this goal allow me to live my values? What values will this expand?

- Will pursuing this goal give me energy for what matters most or deplete it?

- Does this goal honour my authentic needs and talents or reflect others' expectations?

- Will achieving this contribute value to my loved ones and the world?

Evaluating goals through a values lens prevents chasing empty achievements or social validation. Avoid "shoulds" that don't resonate within. When goals align with your essence, the process of achieving them feels inspired.

Integrating Values Into Daily Life

To keep values top of mind, integrate reminders into daily life:

- List your values visibly on your desk, computer wallpaper, bathroom mirror etc.

- Set phone alerts to periodically ask how you are upholding values.

- Share your values with friends/family. Ask them to kindly hold you accountable.

- Notice which activities, places and people reinforce your values. Seek those out.

- Journal moments when you expressed your values to build awareness.

- Collect inspirational quotes, images and music representing your principles. Immerse often.

- Wear symbolic jewellery or accessories denoting important values.

Soon your values will subconsciously guide your thoughts, decisions and behaviours. You'll feel cantered acting from your highest self.

Establishing Values-Based Boundaries

Protect time and energy for what matters by establishing boundaries aligned with values. For example:

- If family is a top value, set parameters on work to be fully present for dinnertime.

- If health matters, commit to consistent sleep and exercise times. Don't let others encroach.

- If service is important, determine reasonable amounts of time, money and resources to dedicate.

Values inevitably conflict some times. For instance, career success may temporarily need balancing against health values. With competing priorities, deeply reflect on the trade-offs of each option aiming for overall balance so no value gets neglected long term.

Updating Values Over Time

Reassess your values continuum as life stages and priorities shift. Set annual reminders to reflect. Ask yourself:

- Have my recent decisions reflected my stated values or have I strayed off course? Do I need to recommit?

- Have my values stayed constant or evolved based on life changes?

- Do I still resonate with past principles or feel called to new ones?

- Do my current values represent my authentic voice or old programming from others?

Be willing to consciously evolve values based on personal growth while retaining core tenets like compassion and wisdom that stand the test of time. Regular recalibration ensures you live your values powerfully.

Defining Your Code of Ethics

Consider drafting a personal code of ethics capturing your core values and principles. This document articulates how you aspire to show up in all areas of life professionally, socially, regarding family, health, community, spirituality, etc. Write it as a binding contract outlining the standards you hold yourself to and revisit it when values feel unclear. Having this code provides a north star amid life's complexities. It reminds you of the person you committed to being at your core when tempted to stray.

Integrating Values into Your Identity

For values to drive your actions subconsciously, integrate them into your self-concept - your beliefs about who you are. Introduce yourself to others using value descriptors. For example, "I'm someone who is passionate about family and community" or "Integrity guides everything I do." Reframe your inner dialogue using value based language. Notice opportunities in conversations to express your principles. Soon your values become automatic, guiding your behaviour without conscious effort because they are woven into your identity. Your principles shape not just your actions but who you are.

The Journey of Self-Discovery

Gaining self-awareness around your authentic values requires courage, honesty and willingness to grow. The reflective journey may surface old pain, unconscious limiting beliefs or expectations absorbed from others. Shedding false programmed values to uncover your essence often means challenging comfort zones. But the quest enables the real you to emerge wiser and more empowered.

Look back on your life's trajectory. What experiences shaped your values? Consider childhood influences, family dynamics, obstacles faced, relationships, successes and failures. Observe the unsung strengths these challenges drew from you. Appreciate how the twists and turns prepared you for deeper purpose.

Then, take stock of who you are today. How do you spend each day? What principles guide your habits and decisions now? Do your present values reflect your core or old conditioning? The gap between your daily reality and aspirational values is the space for your transformation.

Finally, look ahead. How do you wish to grow and contribute meaningfully? Allow your future self to guide you toward who you were always meant to be. Envision your values clearly directing your behavior. Imagine the positive impact you have on the world.

Defining your values requires lifelong curiosity, learning and growth. It is a process, not an endpoint. By regularly reflecting on principles that imbue your life with essence, you return to your highest self again and again. You become who you authentically are. Your values act as compass pointing true north to your unique purpose. With consciousness and consistency, your principles light the path to a values-based life of fulfilment.

Chapter 3: Crafting a Personal Mission Statement

A personal mission statement defines your core purpose and provides a compass to guide your goals and actions. It succinctly encapsulates your passions, values, talents, and aspirations. In this chapter, we will explore what comprises an impactful mission statement, step-by-step guidance for crafting your own, and example case studies to spark reflection on your life's direction and meaning. Defining your mission provides clarity, motivation, and alignment to fuel your personal growth journey.

Understanding Personal Mission Statements

A personal mission statement is a short written paragraph summarizing your driving purpose in life. It captures your unique contribution and essence. While general vision statements describe the future you envision, mission statements focus on the present path to get there. An effective personal mission statement includes:

- Values: Your core principles and ethics.
- Passions: What energizes and excites you.
- Talents: Your natural abilities and strengths.
- Goals: Your aspirations and dreams.
- Purpose: How you serve the world and others.
- Personality: The qualities that make you who you are.

A concise mission statement can be recited from memory and internalized. It provides a decision filter for choices small and large. It gives direction through seasons of change and growth. Defining this mission provides the foundation for living an engaged, meaningful life.

Crafting Your Personal Mission Statement

Be thoughtful and honest as you craft the words that will guide your days on earth. Here is a step-by-step process:

1. Identify your core values. What principles are non-negotiable to you?
2. Get clear on passions that spark joy and energy. When do you lose track of time?

3. Assess your natural talents and strengths. What do you excel at with ease?
4. Set inspiring goals for the next 5-10 years. How will you grow and contribute?
5. Consider your legacy. What impact do you want to leave?
6. Describe your unique personality. What qualities define you?
7. Synthesize key elements into concise, powerful sentences.
8. Craft an inspiring, memorable mission statement that energizes you.
9. Review and refine annually as your purpose evolves.
10. Share your mission with supportive loved ones to actualize it.

While the process requires self-reflection, the resulting mission statement is active and outward-focused. It compels you to share your gifts rather than navel-gaze. A mission statement is not a static document but rather a living compass to align your journey.

Example Personal Mission Statements

Here are examples of diverse mission statements to spark ideas for crafting your own unique purpose:

"To create beautiful, functional art and design that improves people's daily lives." - **Interior Designer**

"To build collaborative teams that innovate systems advancing humanity." - **Social Entrepreneur**

"To leverage my natural curiosity in service of deeply understanding clients' needs and creating tailored solutions." – **Consultant**

"To nurture the potential of each child through joyful learning experiences." – **Teacher**

"To protect and empower those unable to advocate for themselves." - **Social Justice Lawyer**

"To explore diverse cultures and perspectives while fostering intercultural exchange." - **Travel Writer**

"To apply my analytical skills to investigate injustices and systemic issues." - **Investigative Journalist**

"To listen with an open heart and uplift others through motivational storytelling." - **Podcast Host**

"To live simply, consciously, and gratefully while inspiring others to appreciate the beauty around them." - **Mindfulness Guide**

"To passionately lead people and organizations to transform vision into reality." - **Executive Coach**

As exemplified above, mission statements are unique to each individual based on their values, talents, and aspirations. Yours will capture the intersection of who you are and how you contribute to the world.

Integrating Your Mission Statement Into Daily Life
For your mission statement to truly guide your path, integrate it into your daily life:

- Memorize it like a mantra so it becomes engrained in your mind
- Post it visibly on your mirror, desktop, or phone wallpaper
- Share it with friends and family to strengthen your commitment

- Review it when making major life decisions to ensure alignment
- Reflect on it during challenges to reconnect with purpose
- Use it when introducing yourself to explain what drives you
- Measure goals and daily progress against it rather than outside standards
- Allow it to evolve with life stages but retain your essence

Soon your mission will flow from you naturally. It will influence the way you speak, spend time, make decisions, and define success. Each small choice will build incrementally toward your overarching purpose.

Defining Your Mission Liberates Your Potential
Society often tries to prescribe our purpose. Well-intended parents, teachers, and partners project expectations upon us that may not align with our inner truth. Media and marketing define narrow versions of success fueled by status and materialism. The noise of outside voices can silence the call of our own soul.

That is why crafting your personal mission statement is so powerful. It tunes out these distractions so you can hear your inner wisdom. Your mission is for you alone. It already exists as your life's blueprint - your gift is discovering and honouring it. When your days align with this unique purpose, you gain freedom, fulfilment and the joy of actualizing your full potential.

Chapter 4: Setting SMART Goals

Goals that meet the SMART criteria are powerful drivers of success. SMART stands for **Specific, Measurable, Achievable, Relevant,** and **Time-Bound**. This chapter will provide strategies for establishing SMART goals across different areas of your life along with tips to break big goals down into manageable steps. With focused effort on thoughtful SMART goals, you can make steady progress toward realizing your full potential.

Introducing SMART Goals

SMART is an acronym that outlines crucial criteria for setting effective goals:

Specific - Well-defined with details, scope, and requirements. Not vague aspirations but concrete targets.

Measurable - Includes quantifiable metrics and indicators to track progress.

Achievable - Within your capacity, given available skills, resources, and constraints. Reach requires stretch outside comfort zone but not unrealistic expectations.

Relevant - Aligned with your core values, life vision, and current priorities.

Time-Bound - Specified target date or deadline creates needed structure, urgency, and accountability.

SMART goals provide clarity while also offering flexibility to adapt as circumstances evolve. They build momentum by focusing effort on what matters most to you right now.

Setting SMART Career Goals

Meaningful work is essential to actualization. But simply having a job you enjoy is not enough - you must actively sculpt your career path through SMART goals that leverage your strengths in pursuit of your passions.

If looking to switch careers, set SMART goals like:

- By December 2023, create a LinkedIn profile and engage with 25 professionals in my desired new field to learn industry skills and norms.

- By June 2024, take 2 online courses on topics critical for my new career to build expertise.

To excel in your current role, set SMART development goals like:

- By Q3 this year, shadow project leaders successfully managing complex initiatives to learn and document best practices I can adopt.

- By year-end, refine my presentation skills by practicing key pitches 15 times and soliciting manager feedback on delivery style and compelling narrative techniques.

To achieve leadership ambitions, set SMART promotion goals like:

- By mid-2024, spearhead 2 cross-functional projects from concept to completion, demonstrating my ability to deliver results through matrix collaboration.

Whatever your career aims, break down into step-by-step SMART goals that create the competencies and track record for advancement.

Setting SMART Financial Goals

While money alone does not create happiness, financial security provides freedom to pursue your purpose. Set SMART money goals that align with your values like:

- By first quarter next year, pay off $5000 in credit card debt by allocating 15% of monthly income toward balances.

- By 2025, save $20,000 for a downpayment on a home by automatically depositing $400 each month into a separate savings account.

- By age 40, have $500,000 saved for retirement by investing 15% of salary into a 401k and passive index funds.

Outline specific amounts to save or pay down by target dates based on a realistic budget. Constantly chip away at SMART financial milestones.

Setting SMART Health Goals

Your physical and mental wellbeing provides the energy to fully show up each day. Set SMART goals that optimize self-care like:

- Walk 10,000 steps daily for 3 months tracked by a fitness device to lower cholesterol 30 points.

- journal nightly for 2 months to reduce stress and practice mindfulness, scoring mood on a 1-10 scale.

- Meal prep every Sunday to enable eating 5 vegetable servings daily this month, taking vitamins to address nutritional gaps.

Even small incremental health gains compound, so persist with SMART wellness goals.

Setting SMART Relationship Goals

Meaningful connection with others requires continual nurturing. Set SMART relationship-building goals like:

- Schedule biweekly date nights with my partner this quarter to reconnect without distractions, openly communicating on relationship health.

- Have a deep one-on-one conversation with each parent every month this year to strengthen bonds and express appreciation.

- Initiate meetups with 2 friends per month for 6 months to cultivate a trusted social circle and avoid isolation.

SMART relationship goals tailor quality bonding time with those who matter.

Setting SMART Personal Growth Goals

Learning, creating, and exploring new horizons expand your human potential. Set SMART self-actualization goals like:

- Read one book every 2 weeks this year on topics including spirituality, biographies of inspiring figures, art history, and personal development.

- Practice guitar 30 minutes daily for 6 months to gain proficiency, then join a local band to connect with fellow musicians.

- Visit 3 new museums and 2 theater performances this quarter to soak in culture and perspectives different than my own.

Try new activities, engage with thought-provoking media, and push boundaries through SMART personal growth goals.

Sustaining Motivation With SMART Goals

The SMART criteria combat procrastination by creating accountability and urgency. Measurable progress keeps motivation high even during challenging pursuits. Time-bound completion dates anchor you amid the discomfort of change and growth.

SMART goals enable big dreams by linking them to defined incremental wins. Aligning goals with your values and mission ensures the journey remains purposeful and fulfilling. Adjust milestones as needed while retaining the end vision. With consistent SMART goal-setting and follow-through, your life possibilities exponentially expand.

Chapter 5: Prioritizing Based on Impact

With seemingly endless responsibilities and opportunities vying for attention, prioritizing what matters most is an essential productivity skill. This chapter will explore how to filter priorities based on potential return on investment, delegate or remove less critical items, and focus efforts on high-impact goals for maximum effectiveness. Aligning output with meaningful outcomes enables you to make the most of limited time and energy.

Defining True Priorities

The word "priority" gets thrown around loosely. True priorities represent the handful of objectives that would have significant positive impact if you focused effort on them. Recognize that you cannot do everything. Trying to juggle too many priorities leads to scattershot efforts and diluted results. To determine authentic priorities:

- Connect to your core values, mission and current life stage needs. What hopes and responsibilities demand focus now?

- Consider potential return on investment. Where could targeted effort yield exponential benefits? What outcomes would ripple through other areas of life?

- Weigh importance versus urgency. Just because a task demands immediate attention doesn't mean it is truly vital and impactful. Learn to distinguish between the two.

- Observe patterns where small amounts of time invested have generated sizable rewards. Apply "80/20 rule" thinking.

Once you narrow down key priorities, commit without reservation. Say no to distractions outside these laser-focused areas to protect your time, energy, and sanity. Set boundaries and enlist others' support to uphold priorities when tempted to waiver.

Evaluating Where You Currently Spend Time

Before determining where to direct more focus, honestly evaluate how you currently spend time:

- Track all your tasks and activities over the course of one full week.

- Gauge whether each activity aligned with priorities, offered a moderate return, or provided limited value. Be brutally honest with labels.

- Notice in what areas the most time was invested. Do these reflect your actual priorities or default routine?

- Calculate the percentage of time spent proactively on priorities versus reactively on lower value tasks.

Gaining awareness of how you fritter away focus empowers you to change habits and demonstrate your values through priorities.

Mitigating Distractions

Modern life presents unlimited distractions sabotaging priorities. To overcome these:

- When working, block websites and apps that lure you into rabbit holes.

- Set phone boundaries, putting it in another room when concentration is required.

- Schedule a set time to check messages and notifications to prevent constant disruption.

- Communicate to others that certain times are sacrosanct for uninterrupted priority work.

- Notice when you gravitate toward easier busywork that provides comfort versus tackling harder priorities requiring mental stamina.

- Be wary of false urgency that allows minor obligations to override priorities. Let non-critical items wait.

- Institute co-working blocks where you silently work alongside a friend or partner for peer accountability.

With diligence, you can create necessary space to direct focus where it truly matters.

Eliminating and Outsourcing

Free up capacity for priorities by pruning obligations providing limited meaning or impact. Take a close look at your typical commitments:

- Which could you eliminate without negative consequences? What meetings, tasks, and activities could you cut?

- Which provide some value but not enough to warrant your precious focus? Delegate them if feasible.

- What meaningful priorities could you outsource parts of to trusted others? Consider a virtual assistant.

- If eliminating something entirely feels drastic, could you reduce its frequency?

Actively remove anything detracting from priorities to amplify your effectiveness. Be willing to let go of comfortable yet unfulfilling routines.

Execute on Priorities

Carving out space for priorities means little without execution. To excel:

- Break intimidating priority projects into daily bite-sized tasks to create momentum.

- Limit daily priority tasks to 5 or fewer so you can actually complete them versus becoming overwhelmed by a long list.

- Rank daily priorities so that if you only finish the top 1-3, at least those had maximum impact.

- Tackle priorities during peak energy times when your concentration and willpower are highest.

- Match big picture priorities to aligned daily habits that incrementally move you forward.

By structuring days purposefully around clear priorities, your efforts stay focused on what matters at each season of life, compounding to create meaning and fulfilment.

Recalibrating Priorities Over Time

Priorities are not permanently set but rather evolve as goals are met, new opportunities arise, and personal needs shift. Reassess priorities quarterly or yearly to ensure alignment with values and growth. Reflect on what provided a sense of meaning and purpose over the past season and what now calls for focus. Permit your priorities to mature while retaining commitment to overarching lifelong principles. With frequent recalibration, priorities act not as burden but as guide toward your best possible life.

By learning to identify, protect, and execute on only the most vital priorities, you gain freedom from constant overload and overwhelm. Your capabilities flourish because they can be fully invested in the activities that bring significance and joy. The path forward unclouds. With purposeful effort directed toward present priorities, your daily life and long term goals transform.

Chapter 6: Creating a Weekly Schedule.

Effectively managing your time is essential to maximizing productivity and living purposefully. A weekly schedule provides structure that aligns time use with your priorities and values. This chapter will provide a step-by-step guide for thoughtfully planning your week as well as strategies to build daily efficiency. With intention and consistency, your weekly schedule will become a tool for eliminating chaos and maximizing personal effectiveness.

Introducing Time Management

Time is life's great equalizer - we all have 24 hours each day, 168 hours each week. How we choose to spend it determines our effectiveness, happiness, and life outcomes. Time management enables intentionally directing your hours toward priorities rather than reacting haphazardly to each day. Benefits include:

- Increased productivity and progress on meaningful goals

- Reduced stress and overwhelm when life feels under control

- Improved work-life balance when personal needs are scheduled

- Greater ability to anticipate and prepare for known commitments

- More opportunities to relax and rejuvenate when work is contained

When you take command of your schedule, you take command of your life. You transition from passive passenger to active driver determining your direction. But beware perfectionism. Effective time management works for you rather than imposing unrealistic standards. Consistency matters more than meticulous adherence. Use the below tips to develop a weekly schedule serving your needs and gifts.

Reflect on Your Priorities and Habits

Before scheduling your week, reflect on current priorities and habits:

- What 1-3 major goals demand focus and urgency this season of life? How much dedicated time do they require?

- What daily or weekly habits align with your core values and create balance? Examples may include exercise, connecting with loved ones, pursuing hobbies, community service, self-reflection, etc.

- What regular appointments, meetings, and classes need inclusion? These set parameters.

Consider both one-time priorities like a work project as well recurring habits that rejuvenate you. Allocating time for both intentional work and intentional rest boosts wellbeing.

Map Out Fixed Commitments

Start constructing your weekly schedule by recording all fixed commitments first:

- Note regular work hours, commute times, and recurring meetings.

- Add standing appointments like medical checkups, therapy sessions, book club, etc.

- Include sporadic bookings that arise like special events and meetups with friends.

- Schedule errands and household obligations that require designated time, like grocery shopping, laundry, etc.

Blocking these non-negotiable items first provides a template of available time remaining each day/week. See your calendar as a finite resource to allocate wisely.

Schedule Priorities and Habits

Now deliberately schedule your priorities and preferred habits within the windows of availability:

- Assign tasks to complete priority projects during your peak energy and focus times for efficiency.

- Ensure daily movement and exercise by booking fitness classes, walk breaks, etc. Schedule recreation too.

- Dedicate one weekend morning to meal prep and household chores for the week ahead.

- Protect a daily unwinding routine like reading or bath time to transition from work mode to relaxation.

Strive for balance each day between work, relationships, self-care, development. Your schedule should align with your values and meaning.

Minimize Inefficiency

Build in time buffers between activities in case one runs long. Cluster related tasks together when possible, such as making all work phone calls back-to-back. Schedule focus work during periods of minimal interruptions. Say no to overbooking yourself. Protect at least one totally free day per week for flexibility. Beat inefficient use of time through mindful advanced planning.

Iterate as Needed.

Review your weekly schedule to ensure it feels purposeful yet realistic. Make adjustments if meetings were double-booked, you neglected self-care, or allocated insufficient time for priorities. Perfection matters less than thoughtfully striving to align time use with your highest good each day. With practice, managing your schedule will feel empowering rather than restrictive. You will find time for what matters when you intentionally map it out.

Chapter 7: Reflecting on Personal Values and Principles

Our values and principles serve as an inner compass, guiding our choices and shaping our actions. When aligned with core values, life takes on greater meaning, purpose and direction. This chapter provides practical exercises to gain clarity on your values along with techniques to integrate them into daily life. By consciously defining and living your values, you can steer your life toward fulfilment.

Understanding Personal Values

Values represent our highest priorities and deeply held beliefs about what is right, important and meaningful. They reflect the essence of who we are at our core and point to our unique purpose in the world. Values encompass various life domains:

Relationships – How we connect with others

Growth & Contribution – How we challenge ourselves and uplift others

Health & Wellbeing – How we care for our body, mind and spirit

Integrity & Ethics – How we operate with honesty, authenticity and morality

Community & Environment – How we positively engage with the world around us

Achievement & Success – How we apply our talents to reach goals and serve society

Spirituality & Meaning – How we find inner peace, wisdom and connection to the divine

Our values motivate us, bring joy and imbue life with meaning. They guide how we invest our limited time, energy and resources. When facing difficult dilemmas, our values point the way forward. They anchor us through hardships and humbly guide us through triumphs. Our values keep us aligned with life's essence.

Discovering Your Core Personal Values

With so many values to potentially integrate, how can you determine which resonate most deeply? The following reflective exercises can help identify your true north principles:

Recall peak experiences when you felt aligned, joyful and fully yourself. What values do those moments reflect? What activities bring out your best self? If you felt that way more often, what would you do differently?

Consider who and what you appreciate most in life. What do your loved ones, passions, possessions and sanctuaries represent? What makes you feel grounded?

Remember difficult times when you demonstrated resilience. What values empowered you through challenges? What gave you strength and meaning?

Envision your best possible self in 5-10 years. What principles guide your future growth? How do you positively contribute?

Imagine you had one year left to live. How would you spend it? Who and what would matter most? What would give you comfort?

What world issues inspire passion in you? What change would you like to see? How can you be part of the solution?

Once you review these reflections, narrow down 5-10 that form your core essence and align with your life vision. These values become your decision-making filter moving forward.

Assessing Alignment of Values and Actions

With core values defined, assess how consistently your current actions align. Observe your daily routines, habits, conversations and spending:

Do you devote time and energy to activities linked to your values or less important matters?

Do you prioritize self-care in line with your health values or neglect needs?

Does your work fulfil your growth values or drain you?

Do you model integrity through honesty and accountability or bend rules for convenience?

Does your social circle share your values and bring out your best self?

Do you spend money wisely on what matters or mindlessly consume?

Do you uphold spiritual values like mindfulness and gratitude daily or just when remembered?

Misalignment between values and actions signals necessary change. If life feels adrift, you have drifted from your core. Reconnecting to your principles will reignite peace and purpose.

Setting Goals Aligned with Values

With clarified values, set goals exemplifying them so daily efforts build toward your vision. Ensure each goal aligns with core priorities by asking:

How will this goal allow me to live my values? What values will this expand?

Will pursuing this goal give me energy for what matters most or deplete it?

Does this goal honor my authentic needs and talents or reflect others' expectations?

Will achieving this contribute value to my loved ones and the world?

Evaluating goals through a values lens prevents chasing empty achievements or social validation. Avoid "shoulds" that don't resonate within. When goals align with your essence, the process of achieving them feels inspired.

Integrating Values Into Daily Life

To keep values top of mind, integrate reminders into daily life:

List your values visibly on your desk, computer wallpaper, bathroom mirror etc.

Set phone alerts to periodically ask how you are upholding values.

Share your values with friends/family. Ask them to kindly hold you accountable.

Notice which activities, places and people reinforce your values. Seek those out.

Journal moments when you expressed your values to build awareness.

Collect inspirational quotes, images and music representing your principles. Immerse often.

Wear symbolic jewelry or accessories denoting important values.

Soon your values will subconsciously guide your thoughts, decisions and behaviors. You'll feel cantered acting from your highest self.

Establishing Values-Based Boundaries

Protect time and energy for what matters by establishing boundaries aligned with values. For example:

If family is a top value, set parameters on work to be fully present for dinnertime.

If health matters, commit to consistent sleep and exercise times. Don't let others encroach.

If service is important, determine reasonable amounts of time, money and resources to dedicate.

Values inevitably conflict some times. For instance, career success may temporarily need balancing against health values. With competing priorities, deeply reflect on the trade-offs of each option aiming for overall balance so no value gets neglected long term.

Updating Values Over Time

Reassess your values continuum as life stages and priorities shift. Set annual reminders to reflect. Ask yourself:

Have my recent decisions reflected my stated values or have I strayed off course? Do I need to recommit?

Have my values stayed constant or evolved based on life changes?

Do I still resonate with past principles or feel called to new ones?

Do my current values represent my authentic voice or old programming from others?

Be willing to consciously evolve values based on personal growth while retaining core tenets like compassion and wisdom that stand the test of time. Regular recalibration ensures you live your values powerfully.

Defining Your Code of Ethics

Consider drafting a personal code of ethics capturing your core values and principles. This document articulates how you aspire to show up in all areas of life professionally, socially, regarding family, health, community, spirituality, etc. Write it as a binding contract outlining the standards you hold yourself to and revisit it when values feel unclear. Having this code provides a north star amid life's complexities. It reminds you of the person you committed to being at your core when tempted to stray.

Integrating Values into Your Identity

For values to drive your actions subconsciously, integrate them into your self-concept – your beliefs about who you are. Introduce yourself to others using value descriptors. For example, "I'm someone who is passionate about family and community" or "Integrity guides everything I do." Reframe your inner dialogue using value based language. Notice opportunities in conversations to express your principles. Soon your values become automatic, guiding your behavior without conscious effort because they are woven into your identity. Your principles shape not just your actions but who you are.

The Journey of Self-discovery.

Gaining self-awareness around your authentic values requires courage, honesty and willingness to grow. The reflective journey may surface old pain, unconscious limiting beliefs or expectations absorbed from others. Shedding false programmed values to uncover your essence often means challenging comfort zones. But the quest enables the real you to emerge wiser and more empowered.

Look back on your life's trajectory. What experiences shaped your values? Consider childhood influences, family dynamics, obstacles faced, relationships, successes and failures. Observe the unsung strengths these challenges drew from you. Appreciate how the twists and turns prepared you for deeper purpose.

Then, take stock of who you are today. How do you spend each day? What principles guide your habits and decisions now? Do your present values reflect your core or old conditioning? The gap between your daily reality and aspirational values is the space for your transformation.

Finally, look ahead. How do you wish to grow and contribute meaningfully? Allow your future self to guide you toward who you were always meant to be. Envision your values clearly directing your behaviour. Imagine the positive impact you have on the world.

Defining your values requires lifelong curiosity, learning and growth. It is a process, not an endpoint. By regularly reflecting on principles that imbue your life with essence, you return to your highest self again and again. You become who you authentically are. Your values act as compass pointing true north to your unique purpose. With consciousness and consistency, your principles light the path to a values-based life of fulfilment. **In the next chapter we delve into some additional factors for Enhanced Effectiveness**

Chapter 8: Continuous Learning and Personal Development

In today's fast-paced world, the skills and knowledge that made you successful yesterday may not be enough to keep you successful tomorrow. The most successful leaders and organizations recognize the importance of continuous learning and personal development to stay competitive, adaptable, and innovative.

This chapter will provide a comprehensive explanation of continuous learning and personal development, including definitions, benefits, challenges, strategies, and examples. By committing to lifelong learning and growth, you can future-proof your career, add value to your organization, and reach your full potential as a leader.

Definitions

Continuous learning is the ongoing, voluntary pursuit of knowledge and skills that relates to one's personal or professional goals. It involves regularly seeking out new information to expand one's knowledge and skills over time. Personal development is the conscious effort to improve and grow as an individual. It involves activities that strengthen your talents and potential and support your overall wellbeing.

Continuous learning and personal development are linked because expanding one's knowledge and competencies through learning aids overall growth and development. However, personal development is broader in scope as it includes developing non-cognitive abilities like emotional intelligence and creativity.

Benefits

Committing to continuous learning and personal growth provides many benefits for leaders and organizations:

- Staying Relevant - Continuous learning helps leaders stay up-to-date on trends, technologies, and innovations that may disrupt or enhance their industries. This allows them to adapt quickly and make informed decisions.

- Boosting Employability - Leaders who engage in regular skills development are more employable and have expanded career opportunities. This provides job security and flexibility.

- Uncovering New Ideas - Learning exposes leaders to diverse ideas, experiences, and insights that can spark innovation. Fresh perspectives help avoid insular group thought.

- Enhancing Decision-Making - Leaders who expand their knowledge have more data points to draw on when weighing options and making decisions. More informed decisions tend to be better ones.

- Improving Leadership Skills - Leadership skills can always be strengthened. Continuous development enhances emotional intelligence, communication, collaboration, and strategic thinking.

- Driving Organizational Growth - Organizations benefit from the new ideas and increased productivity of learning leaders. Skills development also boosts talent retention.

- Achieving Personal Fulfilment - Continuous learning enables individuals to satisfy their curiosity, actualize their potential, and feel a sense of personal accomplishment.

Challenges

While critical, continuous development presents some challenges that leaders must proactively address:

- Finding Time - Busy schedules make carving out time for learning difficult. Leaders must purposefully prioritize development.

- Maintaining Motivation - Interest in development may wane over time. Leaders must intentionally cultivate their motivation to learn.

- Measuring Impact - Translating knowledge into measurable individual and organizational performance improvements can be difficult. Clear metrics are key.

- Generating Support - Employees may be resistant to culture changes prompted by new ideas. Leadership must effectively communicate the "why" behind development.

- Overcoming Bias - Leaders may dismiss or devalue new information that challenges deeply-held assumptions. Maintaining an open mindset is crucial.

Strategies

Leaders can employ several proven strategies to maximize the benefits and minimize the challenges of continuous learning and personal development:

- Schedule Regular Time - Block off set days and times each week for learning. Consistency is key - treat development time as importantly as other meetings.

- Set Tangible Goals - Identify specific skills to build or knowledge gaps to fill with targeted completion dates to maintain focus and measure progress.

- Curate Relevant Content - Seek out a mix of content explicitly tied to current and desired skills, knowledge, and performance goals. Avoid random, irrelevant content.

- Reflect and Apply - Connect new concepts to current realities. Regularly reflect on learnings and purposefully experiment applying them. Real-world application accelerates development.

- Expand Your Network - Surround yourself with people who have diverse backgrounds, experiences, and ideas. Engage via social media, events, mentorships. New perspectives stimulate new thinking.

- Teach What You Learn - Teaching others consolidates learning and multiplies impact. Deliver training, mentoring, and community talks to share knowledge.

- Make It Social - Learning with others provides accountability, encouragement, and opportunities to share insights. Join peer learning groups online or offline.

- Measure And Track - Quantify improvements in individual and organizational performance tied to learnings. Analyse data to double down on what works and adjust what does not.

- Celebrate Progress - Recognize milestones achieved. Take pride in positive changes realized. Celebrate small steps that eventually add up to giant leaps.

Examples and Case Studies

Some real-world examples illustrate the power of continuous learning and personal development in action:

James Dyson, Inventor and Founder of Dyson

- Committed to continuous hands-on experimentation and learning about engineering, materials science, and manufacturing processes.

- Dyson's persistence led to over 5,000 prototypes before successfully developing the bagless vacuum.

- Ongoing technology development has fuelled consistent growth and industry leadership for Dyson.

Tobi Lütke, CEO of Shopify

- Maintains a "growth mindset" focused on constant personal improvement.

- Devotes at least a month per year to enhancing his leadership skills through intensive learning.

- Reads about 100 books annually across diverse disciplines to fuel innovation and strategic thinking.

- Credits commitment to lifelong learning to his entrepreneurial success.

MasterClass

- Edtech company providing online classes taught by experts across arts, business, fashion, sports.

- Courses enable skills development for career changers, entrepreneurs, creatives, and professionals.

- Users cite career advancement, improved performance, and personal growth realized through MasterClass courses.

- The platform democratizes access to continuous learning from top masters.

Conclusion

The world will continue evolving rapidly, and leadership demands will change with it. Committing now to continuous learning and personal growth equips leaders to steer change confidently, capitalize on emerging opportunities, and thrive in unpredictable futures.

The most successful leaders view learning as a lifelong journey rather than a destination. They instil a culture of learning across their organizations. Although learning efforts may ebb and flow, the quest for improvement never stops. No matter one's current skill level, there is always more growth ahead if we remain open, curious, and determined to realize our full potential.

Chapter 9:

The Benefits of Regular Self-Assessment and Reflection.

In the rush of daily life and work, it's easy to get caught up in the busyness of doing without taking time to reflect on learning and growth. But building in time for regular self-assessment and reflection provides leaders with invaluable benefits that ultimately enhance personal and organizational success.

This chapter will provide a comprehensive look at self-assessment and reflection, including definitions, reasons to make it a priority, strategies to put it into practice, and real-world examples of the positive impacts. You will gain an understanding of how taking time for purposeful self-analysis supports continuous improvement, self-awareness, and optimal performance.

Definitions

Self-assessment is the process of frequently and objectively evaluating and appraising oneself across a range of performance areas, skills, behaviours, and competencies. Reflection is the regular practice of thinking deeply about past actions, decisions, and experiences in order to extract key learnings and insights.

Self-assessment provides concrete data points for reflection. Reflection turns those data points into usable lessons and wisdom. Together, these practices reinforce each other to drive positive change.

Reasons to Prioritize Self-Assessment and Reflection

Dedicated time for self-assessment and reflection benefits leaders in the following ways:

- It illuminates strengths to leverage and weaknesses to improve. You cannot optimize what you do not analyse.

- It increases self-awareness about personal tendencies, work styles, and motivations.

- It enables setting smarter goals based on a realistic baseline.

- It surfaces overlooked mistakes to avoid repeating.

- It reveals gaps between intentions and impact to realign actions with values.

- It grounds decisions and direction in accurate data versus assumptions.

- It boosts learning agility to pivot in dynamic business conditions.

- It enhances emotional intelligence and empathy when applied to understanding others.

- It inspires creativity as reflections generate new solutions.

- It creates a sense of progress by documenting growth over time.

In summary, regular self-focused analysis enhances clarity, learning, course correction, and overall mindset.

Strategies for Effectively Practicing Self-Assessment and Reflection

To reap the many rewards, leaders should employ the following best practices:

- Schedule dedicated time. Book regular appointments on your calendar to ensure self-analysis receives priority time, not just leftover time.

- Ask insightful questions. Move beyond basic assessments of strengths/weaknesses. Ask thought-provoking questions like: What biases shape my perspectives? How might my decisions impact others differently than intended? What am I overlooking?

- Solicit input from others. Gather impressions from colleagues, managers, mentors, friends to gain outside perspective. Compare with your self-perceptions.

- Use established frameworks. Personality tests, leadership competency models, decision-making frameworks, and cognitive reasoning assessments provide structure.

- Keep it professional. Focus your analysis on skills, behaviours, and attitudes related to performance and leadership abilities versus general self-judgment.

- Be radically honest. Accurate insights only come from doing a brutally honest inventory and assessment versus inflating or avoiding truths.

- Document learnings. Write down key lessons, commitments to change, and follow-ups to track accountability and progress.

- Apply insights quickly. Promptly make course corrections and implement ideas generated so reflections lead to real change.

- Review regularly. Revisiting learnings and insights at set intervals sustains change and fosters continuous growth.

Examples of Self-Assessment Driving Success

Here are some real world examples of leaders strategically using self-focused analysis and reflection to excel:

Jim Collins, business author and consultant

- Takes quarterly solo retreats to reflect on learnings, assumptions, and personal patterns. Uses insights to refine research and writings.

- Self-reflection exercises sparked key insights for books Good to Great and Built to Last.

Peter Drucker, management consultant and educator

- Conducted daily self-assessments on his consulting performance to identify areas for improvement.

- Exercises helped him become "America's foremost pioneer on the theory and practice of management," per Harvard Business Review.

Toyota

- Builds in regular structured reflection for employees through Hansei sessions on the production line.

- Continuous self-assessment fuels employee productivity and company quality gains.

Steve Jobs, Apple co-founder and CEO

- Closely studied his own strengths, weaknesses, and motivations as a leader.

- Self-knowledge allowed him to strategically complement his abilities with others like Tim Cook.

Ray Dalio, Founder of Bridgewater Associates

- Radical transparency practices involve assessing and providing feedback on each other's strengths and weaknesses.

- Intense self-reflection yields high performance that has made Bridgewater the world's largest hedge fund.

Conclusion

Making time for regular self-analysis provides leaders with most things assessments deliver – clarity, focus, course correction, improved performance, and progress tracking.

But even more profoundly, it builds self-awareness, emotional intelligence, and wisdom. These lead to deeper purpose and meaning, richer relationships, and enhanced leadership influence.

While challenging at times, courageously exploring your inner landscape through regular self-assessment and reflection enables the personal breakthroughs that spur professional breakthroughs and lasting fulfilment.

Chapter 10: Emotional Intelligence and Self-Awareness

Emotional intelligence, or EQ, has become a buzzword in leadership development for good reason. Research confirms that it is one of the most powerful drivers of leadership success, even outweighing IQ and technical expertise.

This chapter will provide a deep dive into emotional intelligence and self-awareness. You will gain an understanding of what emotional intelligence entails, its concrete benefits, key competencies, best practices for strengthening it, and real-world examples of it in action. Walk away equipped with strategies to enhance your self-awareness and EQ to maximize your leadership capabilities.

Defining Emotional Intelligence and Self-Awareness

Emotional intelligence refers to the ability to recognize and regulate emotions in yourself and others. It involves being attuned to how people feel and responding appropriately based on that understanding.

Self-awareness is the foundation of emotional intelligence. It means deeply knowing your personal emotions, drivers, strengths, weaknesses, biases and impact on others. Self-awareness enables you to manage yourself effectively and empathize accurately.

Benefits of High Emotional Intelligence and Self-Awareness

Leaders with strong emotional intelligence and self-awareness create measurable valued Self-Awareness

- Making smarter decisions by considering emotional factors along with data points.

- Resolving conflict faster through diplomacy and emotional understanding.

- Reducing staff churn by fostering cultures where people feel valued.

- Unlocking innovation by leveraging diverse thinking powered by trust.

- Enabling growth through influence via compelling vision and empathy.

- Accelerating change by aligning people through self-aware communication.

In short, EQ allows leaders to inspire the best from their people, organizations, and themselves.

Emotional Intelligence Competencies

Experts identify core competencies that comprise overall emotional intelligence:

Self-awareness involves accurately assessing your own emotions, drivers, strengths and weaknesses. Self-management is your ability to regulate your emotional reactions and behaviors constructively.

Social awareness refers to understanding others' perspectives, emotions, concerns, and needs. Relationship management means using emotional insight to interact effectively and empathetically.

Strategies to Increase Emotional Intelligence

Just as emotional intelligence can be learned, it can also be developed. Growth requires commitment, courage and the following strategies:

- Reflect through journalling, meditation and regular self-assessment on feelings, experiences, triggers, and reactions. Increased self-understanding is the foundation.

- Get feedback from others on how you are perceived and your impact to gain outside perspective. Ask about blind spots.

- Observe emotions and body language in real interactions. Analyze what cues and signals you miss.

- Read people's emotions and check your interpretation. Ask "What emotions might you be feeling?"

- Expand empathy through books, films, volunteering. See diverse perspectives.

- Role play challenging interpersonal scenarios to practice constructive responses.

- Improve active listening skills through mirroring, paraphrasing, open-ended questions. Fully focus on understanding others.

- Develop self-care routines to manage stress and avoid burnout. Your EQ decreases when running on empty.

- Surround yourself with emotionally intelligent mentors and friends whose behaviours you can model.

The goal is translating emotional awareness into constructive thoughts, dialogue and actions.

Examples of Emotional Intelligence in Leadership

Here are some examples that illustrate the power of emotional intelligence in the real world:

Maya Angelou, Poet

- Demonstrated exceptional capacity to empathize and connect deeply with others from widely divergent backgrounds.

- Was able to inspire and influence broad audiences through profound emotional understanding.

Google

- EQ valued as an important hiring competency, especially for leaders to unite diverse teams.

- Emotional intelligence training offered to employees to drive collaboration and people development.

Virgin Group

- Founder Sir Richard Branson has spoken extensively about the role of EQ in his success.

- EQ emphasized in management training to create constructive company culture.

Oprah Winfrey, Media Executive and Host

- Credits self-awareness for evolution from impoverished childhood to billionaire business leader.

- Leveraged emotional intelligence to forge intimate bonds with audiences worldwide.

Nelson Mandela, President of South Africa

- Used exceptional understanding of emotions, divides, and social dynamics to unify the nation post-apartheid.

These leaders demonstrate how optimizing EQ enables resonating with people, unifying around vision, driving change and creating lasting legacies.

Conclusion

Emotional intelligence separates the most effective leaders from the average. While IQ and technical skills open doors, EQ allows leaders to fully leverage relationships, talent and opportunities.

Strengthening your capacity to perceive, understand and manage emotions - both your own and others' - remains an endeavor without limit. But committing to daily EQ development brings rewards to celebrate each step of the journey: relationships that flourish, conflict dissolved creatively, diverse people unified around shared vision, influence that drives change and organizations that thrive.

Chapter 11: Book Conclusion

This comprehensive guide explored the foundations for maximizing personal effectiveness and living to your full potential. We covered strategies to tap into your core values and craft an inspiring life vision. With your purpose clarified, you can proactively set goals and make plans that align with what matters most.

To progress each day, defeat procrastination through thoughtful time management, consistent motivation, and organized environments. Be sure to balance focused effort with rejuvenating rest. Reflect often on your values and principles to stay grounded in what gives your life meaning.

At the core, strive for self-awareness through regular assessment, reflection, and emotional intelligence growth. Avoid limiting thoughts and perfectionism. Take ownership of your locus of control. Small daily steps towards self-improvement compound over time.

Beyond foundational strategies, lifelong learning and skills development future-proof your potential. Stay hungry for knowledge across diverse disciplines and perspectives. Teach what you learn to others. Measure and track progress.

No matter how much you have achieved, more growth lies ahead. Approaching life with an abundance mindset opens up possibilities. Your unique talents are meant to be shared generously with the world. Living your purpose is an open-ended endeavour to enjoy.

By consistently taking action aligned with your values and highest priorities, you will reach new levels of meaning, contribution, and fulfillment. With a growth-focused mindset , everyday presents opportunities to better yourself and positively impact others. Your personal journey is yours to consciously create. Define it. Own it. Live it fully.

This comprehensive guide explored the foundations for maximizing personal effectiveness and living to your full potential. We covered strategies to tap into your core values and craft an inspiring life vision. With your purpose clarified, you can proactively set goals and make plans that align with what matters most.

To progress each day, defeat procrastination through thoughtful time management, consistent motivation, and organized environments. Be sure to balance focused effort with rejuvenating rest. Reflect often on your values and principles to stay grounded in what gives your life meaning.

At the core, strive for self-awareness through regular assessment, reflection, and emotional intelligence growth. Avoid limiting thoughts and perfectionism. Take ownership of your locus of control. Small daily steps towards self-improvement compound over time.

Beyond foundational strategies, lifelong learning and skills development future-proof your potential. Stay hungry for knowledge across diverse disciplines and perspectives. Teach what you learn to others. Measure and track progress.

No matter how much you have achieved, more growth lies ahead. Approaching life with an abundance mind-set opens up possibilities. Your unique talents are meant to be shared generously with the world. Living your purpose is an open-ended endeavour to enjoy.

By consistently taking action aligned with your values and highest priorities, you will reach new levels of meaning, contribution, and fulfilment. With a growth-focused mindset, everyday presents opportunities to better yourself and positively impact others. Your personal journey is yours to consciously create. Define it. Own it. Live it fully.

Appendices

Appendix A: Developing Your Personal Vision

1. Clarifying Your Values:

- Think about fulfilling moments and the values they represent.

- Identify people and things you appreciate and what they symbolize.

- Recall challenging times and the values that empowered you.

- Envision your ideal future self and guiding principles.

- Reflect on what would matter most in your last year of life.

- Determine world issues that inspire passion in you.

- Use the Core Values Worksheet template to capture your key values.

2. Crafting Your Life Vision:

- Imagine your ideal future life in detail.

- Identify experiences that would bring deep fulfilment.

- Consider how you want to make an impact on the world.

- Determine key skills and mindsets your future self possesses.

- Synthesize these elements into an inspirational written vision.

- Use the Life Vision Worksheet template to capture vision components.

Recommended Resources:

- "The First 20 Hours: How to Learn Anything Fast" by Josh Kaufman

- "Essentialism: The Disciplined Pursuit of Less" by Greg McKeown

Appendix B: Setting Effective Goals

1. SMART Goal Setting:

- Break down your vision into 1, 3, and 5-year goals.

- Make each goal Specific, Measurable, Achievable, Relevant, and Time-bound.

- Outline quarterly, monthly, and weekly objectives for each goal.

- Align goals with your core values for motivation.

- Anticipate obstacles and develop strategies to overcome them.

- Use the SMART Goals Template to document your goals.

Recommended Resources:

- "Atomic Habits" by James Clear

- "The Progress Principle" by Teresa Amabile

Appendix C: Optimizing Personal Effectiveness

1. Weekly Planning Process:

- Map out fixed commitments and scheduling constraints.

- Schedule priorities and preferred habits.

- Build buffers between activities and cluster related tasks.

- Minimize inefficient use of time through advanced planning.

- Adjust the schedule as needed.

- Use the Ideal Week Schedule template to map out your week.

2. Reflecting on Values:

- Assess daily choices for alignment with core values.

- Identify areas of misalignment that require change.

- Set goals that exemplify your values.

- Keep values top of mind with reminders and reflections.

- Use the Reflecting on My Values Worksheet for self-assessment.

3. Structured Self-Reflection:

- Schedule regular time for reflection.

- Ask probing questions to gain insights.

- Seek input from others for an outside perspective.

- Use frameworks to provide structure.

- Document key learnings and follow-ups.

- Make course corrections based on new insights.

- Use the Self-Reflection Template with reflection questions.

Recommended Resources:

- "Deep Work" by Cal Newport

- "The ONE Thing" by Gary Keller

Appendix D: Growth and Development

1. Continuous Learning:

- Allocate regular time for learning and development.

- Set SMART goals for building skills and gaining knowledge.

- Curate a mix of learning resources tailored to your goals.

- Apply learnings to real-world situations.

- Share knowledge through training and teaching others.

- Use the Personal Development Plan template to capture learning goals.

2. Developing Emotional Intelligence:

- Reflect on emotional patterns and triggers.

- Seek feedback from others on how you are perceived.

- Observe emotional cues and body language in interactions.

- Validate interpretations of others' emotions with curiosity.

- Engage with diverse perspectives.

- Role play challenging interpersonal scenarios.

- Enhance active listening and empathy skills.

- Manage stress through self-care to avoid burnout.

- Model emotionally intelligent mentors and friends.

- Use the EQ Development Plan template to capture EQ goals.

Recommended Resources:

- "The Coaching Habit" by Michael Bungay Stanier

- "Leading with Emotional Intelligence" by Kathy Lubar and Belle Linda Halpern

- Take relevant courses on platforms like LinkedIn Learning, Udemy, Master Class for example.

Further media Resources:

Books:

- - "The Coaching Habit" by Michael Bungay Stanier
- - "Leading with Emotional Intelligence" by Kathy Lubar and Belle Linda Halpern
- The 7 Habits of Highly Effective People by Stephen Covey - Explores finding your voice and purpose as a key habit for effectiveness.
- Essentialism: The Disciplined Pursuit of Less by Greg McKeown - Focuses on living intentionally by design rather than default.
- Big Magic: Creative Living Beyond Fear by Elizabeth Gilbert - Inspires readers to uncover their creative passion and purpose.
- The Desire Map by Danielle LaPorte - A guide to clarifying core desires and aligning life with them.
- The Subtle Art of Not Giving a F*ck by Mark Manson - Counterintuitive take on not

wasting energy on things not connected to your values.

Articles:

- "What is Your Life Purpose? And How to Find It" - Mindvalley blog
- "How to Find Your Passion and Purpose in Life" - Psychology Today
- "How to Write a Personal Mission Statement" - The Balance Careers
- "Living with Purpose: 6 Ways to Find Your Path" - Mayo Clinic Health System

Online Resources:

- projectlifemastery.com - Free course on discovering life purpose
- marieforleo.com - Variety of blogs/videos on living intentionally
- mindvalley.com - Programs on self-awareness and actualization
- ted.com - Talks like "How to get clear on your purpose"

- refinery29.com - Career/life advice including finding passion and meaning

The key is integrating resources that blend timeless wisdom with practical application on charting an inspiring life vision and aligning daily choices accordingly. A combination of philosophical ideals and tactical advice provides a robust toolset.

Printed in Great Britain
by Amazon